THE AMERICAN CIVIL WAR

SLAVERY, EMANCIPATION, AND THE CIVIL WAR

A MyReportLinks.com Book

Kim A. O'Connell

MyReportLinks.com Books

an imprint of

Enslow Publishers, Inc. E

Box 398, 40 Industrial Road
Berkeley Heights, NJ 07922
USA

MyReportLinks.com Books, an imprint of Enslow Publishers, Inc. MyReportLinks®
is a registered trademark of Enslow Publishers, Inc.

Library of Congress Cataloging-in-Publication Data

O'Connell, Kim A.
  Slavery, emancipation, and the Civil War / Kim A. O'Connell.
    p. cm — (The American Civil War)
Summary: Describes the conditions of slaves in the United States, the
role of African Americans in the Civil War, and the aftermath of
slavery. Includes Internet links to Web sites related to the Civil War.
Includes bibliographical references (p.) and index.
  ISBN 0-7660-5190-0
  1. Slavery—United States—History—Juvenile literature. 2.
Slaves—Emancipation—United States—Juvenile literature. 3. United
States—History—Civil War, 1861–1865—African Americans—Juvenile
literature. 4. United States. President (1861–1865 : Lincoln).
Emancipation Proclamation–Juvenile literature. 5. African
Americans–History–Juvenile literature. [1. Slavery–History. 2.
African Americans—History.] I. Title. II. American Civil War (Berkeley
Heights, N.J.)
  E441.O24 2004
  973.7'14—dc22
                                2003018168

Printed in the United States of America

10 9 8 7 6 5 4 3 2 1

To Our Readers:

Through the purchase of this book, you and your library gain access to the Report Links that specifically back up this book.

The Publisher will provide access to the Report Links that back up this book and will keep these Report Links up to date on **www.myreportlinks.com** for three years from the book's first publication date.

We have done our best to make sure all Internet addresses in this book were active and appropriate when we went to press. However, the author and the Publisher have no control over, and assume no liability for, the material available on those Internet sites or on other Web sites they may link to.

The usage of the MyReportLinks.com Books Web site is subject to the terms and conditions stated on the Usage Policy Statement on **www.myreportlinks.com**.

A password may be required to access the Report Links that back up this book. The password is found on the bottom of page 4 of this book.

Any comments or suggestions can be sent by e-mail to comments@myreportlinks.com or to the address on the back cover.

Photo Credits: © Hemera Technologies, Inc., 1997–2001, p. 9; Enslow Publishers, Inc., pp. 23, 32; Library of Congress, pp. 1, 3, 18, 20, 22, 27, 31, 34, 42; MyReportLinks.com Books, pp. 4, back cover; National Archives and Records Administration, pp. 36, 44; PBS, *Africans in America*, pp. 10, 12, 14, 16, 24, 26, 29, 38, 41.

Cover Photo: All images, Library of Congress.

Contents

About MyReportLinks.com Books

MyReportLinks.com Books
Great Books, Great Links, Great for Research!

The Report Links listed on the following four pages can save you hours of research time by **instantly** bringing you to the best Web sites relating to your report topic.

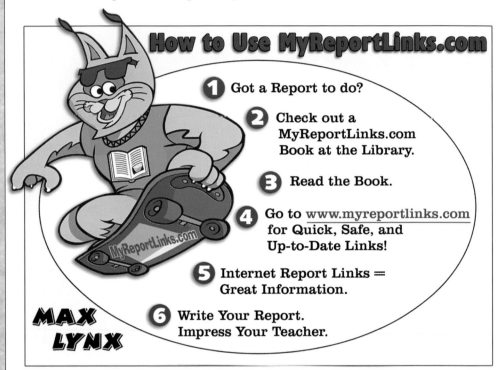

How to Use MyReportLinks.com

1 Got a Report to do?

2 Check out a MyReportLinks.com Book at the Library.

3 Read the Book.

4 Go to www.myreportlinks.com for Quick, Safe, and Up-to-Date Links!

5 Internet Report Links = Great Information.

6 Write Your Report. Impress Your Teacher.

MAX LYNX

The pre-evaluated Web sites are your links to source documents, photographs, illustrations, and maps. They also provide links to dozens—even hundreds—of Web sites about your report subject.

MyReportLinks.com Books and the MyReportLinks.com Web site save you time and make report writing easier than ever!

Please see "To Our Readers" on the copyright page for important information about this book, the MyReportLinks.com Web site, and the Report Links that back up this book. Please enter **WSE6006** if asked for a password.

Report Links

The Internet sites described below can be accessed at
http://www.myreportlinks.com

▶**The American Civil War Homepage**   *EDITOR'S CHOICE
This collection of Civil War Internet resources includes biographies,
facts, images, regiment histories, and fictional accounts of wartime.
Public and private document collections are included.

▶**The Underground Railroad by *National Geographic***   *EDITOR'S CHOICE
This interactive site offers viewers the chance to step into the role of a
slave who is deciding to escape slavery through the Underground
Railroad. Learn about the roles that Harriet Tubman and others played
in leading slaves to freedom.

▶**Documenting the American South**   *EDITOR'S CHOICE
This archival site from the University of North Carolina at Chapel Hill
presents first person narratives of ordinary Southerners from colonial
times through the early twentieth century. African-American slave
narratives are included.

▶**The American Museum of Photography:**   *EDITOR'S CHOICE
The Face of Slavery
This photography collection covers a half century as African Americans
fought slavery and struggled with racism and poverty.

▶**The African-American Mosaic**   *EDITOR'S CHOICE
This online exhibit presents four areas of the African-American Mosaic:
Colonization, Abolition, Migrations, and the Work Projects
Administration. View images, documents, and ex-slave narratives.

▶**Harriet Jacobs**   *EDITOR'S CHOICE
This site contains a brief biography of Harriet Jacobs, who escaped
slavery, and it also includes excerpts from her autobiography *Incidents in
the Life of a Slave Girl.*

Report Links

**The Internet sites described below can be accessed at
http://www.myreportlinks.com**

▶**Aboard the Underground Railroad**

This NPS site includes a map of the Underground Railroad routes that many slaves traveled to freedom. Included is a list of sites, including safe houses, associated with the routes.

▶**Abraham Lincoln Papers at the Library of Congress**

In its online version, the Abraham Lincoln Papers collection comprises approximately 61,000 images and 10,000 transcriptions. You will find transcripts of the Emancipation Proclamation, Gettysburg Address, and many other historical documents.

▶**Africans in America**

This PBS site provides a look at the long and difficult history of Africans in America from colonial times until the end of the Civil War.

▶**Amistad Research Center**

In 1839, fifty-three Africans were abducted from West Africa, in violation of international law, and forced to sail to Cuba aboard *La Amistad* to be sold as slaves. The story of their revolt and struggle to return home, which led them to the United States, is told here.

▶**The Atlantic Slave Trade and Slave Life in the Americas:
A Visual Record**

An image gallery of paintings, drawings, and photos associated with the Atlantic slave trade and slave life in the Americas is provided in this site, which also includes maps and narratives.

▶**The Avalon Project**

This project from the Yale Law School is a collection of documents relevant to law, history, economics, politics, diplomacy, and government. Included on this site are those relating to slavery in America.

▶**Beyond Face Value: Depictions of Slavery in Confederate Currency**

Learn of America's economic history before the Civil War, major events leading up to the war, and view images of Confederate currency depicting slavery.

▶**Born in Slavery: Slave Narratives From the Federal Writers' Project,
1936–1938**

This collection from the Library of Congress contains more than two thousand narratives from former African-American slaves who were interviewed during the 1930s. Archival photographs are also included.

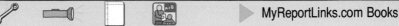
Report Links

The Internet sites described below can be accessed at http://www.myreportlinks.com

▶ **The *Encyclopaedia Britannica* Guide to Black History**

This site offers a time line of black history that includes the beginnings of slavery in America. Also included is an "Eras of Black History" section that chronicles history from the slave revolts of early America through the successes of the civil rights movement.

▶ **Featured Documents: The Emancipation Proclamation**

From the National Archives Web site, you can read the text of the Emancipation Proclamation. Created by President Abraham Lincoln in 1862, this proclamation, issued in 1863, freed the slaves in the states then under rebellion.

▶ **Freedmen's Bureau**

Learn about the establishment and history of the Freedmen's Bureau, a government agency set up after the Civil War to provide short-term relief, including basic shelter and medical care, to former slaves.

▶ **From Revolution to Reconstruction**

This site offers biographies, documents, essays, and more on periods in American history, including biographies and documents related to the history of slavery in America.

▶ **John Brown and the Valley of the Shadow**

This site from the University of Virginia provides narratives, a chronology of events, and newspaper and eyewitness accounts of John Brown's raid on the Harpers Ferry arsenal.

▶ **Harriet Beecher Stowe Center**

Read a biography of the life and times of Harriet Beecher Stowe, whose novel *Uncle Tom's Cabin* strengthened the antislavery sentiment in America.

▶ **In the Valley of the Shadow**

This site offers a unique look at life in two communities, one Northern and the other Southern, during the Civil War. Included are maps, narratives, photographs, and more.

▶ **The Kansas Collection: Bleeding Kansas Gallery**

In the years before the Civil War, Kansas became a battleground between proslavery and antislavery forces. This site offers a look at "Bleeding Kansas" through primary sources and archival materials.

Report Links

The Internet sites described below can be accessed at http://www.myreportlinks.com

▶**The King Center**

The King Center is a living memorial dedicated to the legacy of civil rights leader Dr. Martin Luther King, Jr. The center's Web site includes biographies of Dr. King and his wife, Coretta, as well as archival footage of the civil rights movement and its leaders.

▶**Letters of the Civil War**

This site is a collection of letters, stories, and diaries of American soldiers, sailors, nurses, politicians, ministers, journalists, and citizens during the Civil War.

▶**Library of Congress: The Declaration of Independence**

The Declaration of Independence in its entirety is presented in this Library of Congress site. Although the preamble states that "all men are created equal," the truth was otherwise, especially for African-American slaves.

▶**The Lincoln Institute**

The Lincoln Institute produces and maintains five Web sites that offer scholars, researchers, and the general public a chance to learn more about the life and times of Abraham Lincoln.

▶**Slavery in America**

This comprehensive site designed for educators provides information in many forms on the history of slaves and slavery in America. Maps, paintings and drawings, and photographs are included.

▶**Transatlantic Slavery, Merseyside Maritime Slavery Museum**

This British site takes a look at the Atlantic slave trade. One focus is the "trade triangle," or the combination of European money, African slave labor, and American land that supplied European markets with sugar, coffee, rice, and later, cotton.

▶**University of Oklahoma College of Law: U.S. Historical Documents**

This university site holds American historical documents from the sixteenth century to the present, including those relating to slavery in America.

▶**Washington University Libraries: The Dred Scott Case**

This university site includes an archive of legal and biographical material on Dred Scott, who sued the United States for his freedom. The landmark U.S. Supreme Court ruling in the case found that, among other things, African-American slaves were not U.S. citizens under the Constitution.

Slavery, Emancipation, and the Civil War Facts

1619—The first Africans arrive in Virginia as indentured servants. Soon afterward, slave codes establish the hereditary nature of slavery.

1787—The Northwest Ordinance bans slavery in the Northwest Territory.

1787–1788—The U.S. Constitution establishes the "three-fifths clause," in which only three fifths of slaves are counted in state populations.

1793—The first Fugitive Slave Law is enacted.

1820–1821—The Missouri Compromise bans slavery in lands obtained through the Louisiana Purchase that lie north of the 36° 30′ line of latitude.

1850—The Compromise of 1850 admits California to the Union as a free state, creates a stronger Fugitive Slave Law, and allows territories gained from the Mexican-American War to be organized without mention of slavery.

1852—Harriet Beecher Stowe publishes the antislavery novel *Uncle Tom's Cabin*, which becomes a best-seller.

1854—The Kansas-Nebraska Act admits the territories of Kansas and Nebraska, leaving the question of allowing slavery there to its white settlers.

1855–1856—The "Bleeding Kansas" battles break out between proslavery and antislavery groups.

1857—In the Dred Scott case, the U.S. Supreme Court rules that African Americans are not citizens and do not have civil rights protected by the U.S. Constitution.

1859—John Brown fails to capture a federal arms warehouse at Harpers Ferry, Virginia, to start a slave rebellion.

1860—*Nov.:* Abraham Lincoln, a lawyer from Illinois who is opposed to the spread of slavery, is elected president of the United States. In the months afterward, eleven Southern states withdraw from the Union to form the Confederate States of America.

1861—*April:* The firing on Fort Sumter, South Carolina, begins the Civil War. President Lincoln calls for Union troops to be mobilized.

1862—*Sept.:* Union forces hold their ground in the battle of Antietam in Maryland. Following the Union victory, Lincoln announces a preliminary Emancipation Proclamation.

1863—*Jan. 1:* The Emancipation Proclamation goes into effect, freeing all slaves in the states then under rebellion. African-American regiments in the Union army are quickly formed. Nearly 200,000 black men will serve the Union.

1865—The Civil War ends, with a Union victory.

The Thirteenth Amendment to the Constitution, which formally ends slavery everywhere in the United States, is ratified.

1868—The Fourteenth Amendment to the Constitution is ratified. It guarantees citizenship and related rights to all people born or naturalized in the United States.

1870—The Fifteenth Amendment to the Constitution is ratified. It declares that a person's right to vote cannot be denied on the basis of race, color, or previous condition as a slave.

Escaping to Freedom

In the hot, airless space above a shed that was attached to her grandmother's house, Harriet Jacobs waited and listened. She was stretched out on a bed on the floor, her nose just three feet from the roof of the crawl space. If she turned suddenly, she would hit her head. Rats and mice scurried across the bed in the darkness. Harriet could not tell

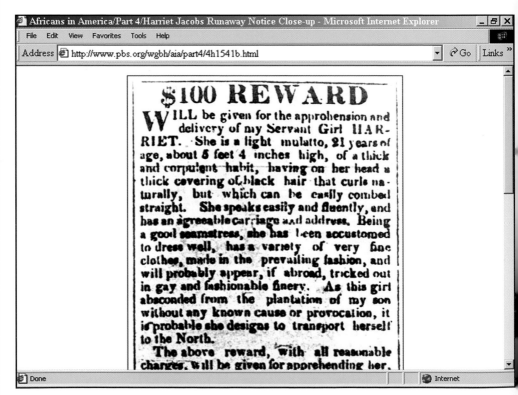

Africans in America/Part 4/Harriet Jacobs Runaway Notice Close-up - Microsoft Internet Explorer

File   Edit   View   Favorites   Tools   Help

Address   http://www.pbs.org/wgbh/aia/part4/4h1541b.html   Go   Links

$100 REWARD

WILL be given for the apprehension and delivery of my Servant Girl HARRIET. She is a light mulatto, 21 years of age, about 5 feet 4 inches high, of a thick and corpulent habit, having on her head a thick covering of black hair that curls naturally, but which can be easily combed straight. She speaks easily and fluently, and has an agreeable carriage and address. Being a good seamstress, she has been accustomed to dress well, has a variety of very fine clothes, made in the prevailing fashion, and will probably appear, if abroad, tricked out in gay and fashionable finery. As this girl absconded from the plantation of my son without any known cause or provocation, it is probable she designs to transport herself to the North.

The above reward, with all reasonable charges, will be given for apprehending her,

Done   Internet

▲ A reward for the capture and return of Harriet Jacobs to her owner promised $100.

whether it was night or day. As she crouched, trying to get comfortable, she strained to hear the voices of her young son and daughter, who were often just outside the house. It was a terrible way to live, but it was better than life as a slave.

Harriet Jacobs had escaped from slavery, but she had not used the mysterious routes of the Underground Railroad. She was hiding on the same North Carolina plantation where she had worked as a slave—and where her master had been threatening to abuse her. Harriet's secret was kept safe by her kindly grandmother, who had been granted her freedom, and an aunt and uncle who lived nearby. Harriet's uncle had built a trapdoor that led up to the attic. The trapdoor became Harriet's lifeline to those relatives. At night, and only at night, she would crawl to the door, through which her family would send food and whisper the latest news. Her master thought that she had escaped to the North, as many other slaves had done. If he knew the truth, Harriet and her family would have been severely punished or killed.

Harriet made the best of her sad situation. "It seemed horrible to sit or lie in a cramped position day after day, without one gleam of light," she later wrote. "Yet I would have chosen this, rather than my lot as a slave. . . ."[1] Harriet knew that her master was not as cruel as some were. Unlike other slaves, Harriet had not been whipped and beaten from head to toe, chained to a heavy log, or branded like cattle. Yet she and her two children had endured many hardships. Harriet was determined to secure her own freedom and, someday, that of her children.

In the meantime, it was enough for her to know that her children were near. Soon after she began hiding in the crawl space, Harriet found a tool stuck in the wall of the shed. She used it to drill a peephole about one inch wide,

through which she could enjoy a little light and fresh air. Every once in a while, she could see the faces of her children outside and hear their voices. Eventually, Harriet, who had been taught to read, learned to hold books or knit in a certain position, to catch whatever light came through the hole. She made clothes and playthings for her children, although they were not allowed to know who made them, for fear that they would reveal her secret. Days turned into months, and months into years.

When she had passed seven years in the tiny crawl space, Harriet heard that plans had been made for her

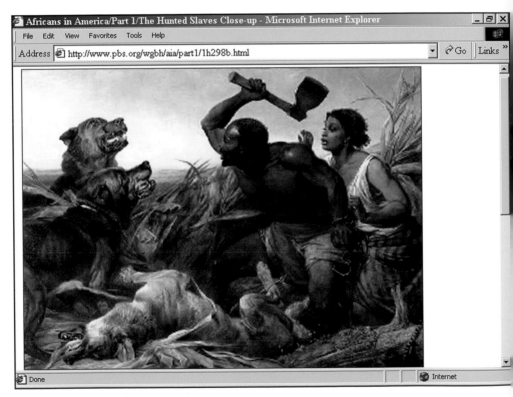

Africans in America/Part 1/The Hunted Slaves Close-up - Microsoft Internet Explorer

File   Edit   View   Favorites   Tools   Help

Address http://www.pbs.org/wgbh/aia/part1/1h298b.html   Go   Links

Done   Internet

▲ This painting, done in the 1860s, dramatizes the plight of escaped African-American slaves, caught in a swamp and surrounded by vicious dogs. Fugitive slave laws made such escape attempts dangerous for both slaves and those who tried to help them.

escape to the North. Under cover of night, she sailed on a small boat that eventually made its way to the Chesapeake Bay. From there, she traveled to Philadelphia and then to New York, where she was eventually reunited with her children, who had also been freed by friends and relatives. But the North had its dangers too. Under the Fugitive Slave Law, slave owners or slave catchers were allowed to cross state lines to recapture their slaves. Harriet's master found the family in New York and vowed to take them back into slavery. Yet Harriet's friends quickly paid off the man, and Harriet and her children were free, once and for all.

Harriet's life as a slave—and her brave journey toward freedom—is just one painful, sad, and yet joyous story in the long history of slavery. Slavery in America dates back to the earliest days of the colonies and ends with the bloody Civil War. Millions of slaves led miserable lives. They suffered injustices at the hands of their masters and were robbed of the most basic freedoms and dignities. Yet thousands of slaves escaped their bondage, often using the Underground Railroad, a network of people and safe houses that helped slaves to find freedom in the North. Some became famous speakers and writers. Harriet Jacobs, for example, wrote *Incidents in the Life of a Slave Girl*, one of the longest slave narratives written by a woman. Others joined the Union army to fight in the Civil War. Whether writing or fighting, they wanted to defend those slaves who could not defend themselves—and offer hope for a future without slavery.

"It has been painful to me, in many ways, to recall the dreary years I passed in bondage," Harriet wrote in her narrative. "[Yet] with those gloomy recollections come tender memories of my good old grandmother, like light, fleecy clouds floating over a dark and troubled sea."[2]

Slavery in America

The seeds of slavery were planted with the very first colonial settlements in the United States. In 1619, the first Africans in the English colonies in America were brought to Virginia as indentured servants. Unlike slaves, indentured servants were promised freedom after they

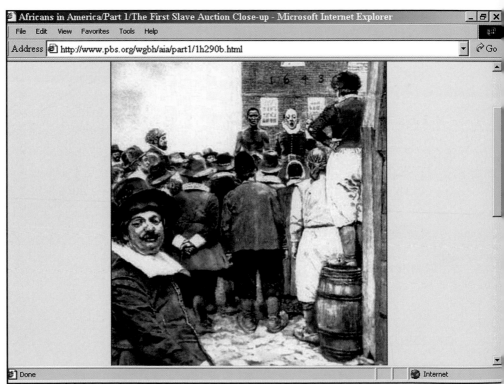

Africans in America/Part 1/The First Slave Auction Close-up - Microsoft Internet Explorer

File Edit View Favorites Tools Help

Address http://www.pbs.org/wgbh/aia/part1/1h290b.html

Done   Internet

▲ This early-twentieth-century painting depicts the first slave auction, in 1655, in New Amsterdam, a town at the tip of Manhattan Island in the Dutch colony of New Netherland. That "town" would later become New York City.

fulfilled the terms of their contract to work. But the people in the colonies soon realized that slavery was a cheap source of labor, and they wanted to maintain the practice. By the late seventeenth century, the colonies had established laws stating that African Americans and their offspring were slaves for life.

In 1776, during the American Revolution, the nation's forefathers adopted the Declaration of Independence. Its famous preamble states that "all men are created equal," but "all men" did not include African slaves.

The Life of a Slave

Slaves were denied the most basic human freedoms. Slave children, for example, were not allowed to know their birthdays or to attend school. Slaves often got married—"Jumping the broom" in the African tradition—but these slave marriages meant nothing to slaveholders. (Since slaves could not legally marry, they created their own marriage rituals. Jumping over a broom signified the sweeping away of the old life and the joining together in marriage of two lives.) Slave codes did not allow slaves to leave the plantation without permission, hit a white person (even in self-defense), buy and sell items, or visit the homes of whites or free blacks.

Many slaves spent their days working as field hands on plantations—usually cotton plantations in the Deep South. Men and women, teenagers and adults, worked side by side in the fields, planting and harvesting crops. Children were even put to work, pulling weeds and fetching water for other workers. Other slaves acted as servants in the main house, seeing to their owners' every need. Slave women often sewed, cooked, and took care of the children—both black and white.

Treatment of slaves was different from plantation to plantation. Some owners were cruel taskmasters who beat their slaves if they were late to the fields or did not perform their work in a certain way. Slave families were torn apart when members were sold to different plantations, often far away. At other plantations, some slaves received better treatment. In some cases, owners eventually freed their slaves or allowed their freedom to be bought for the right price.

Whenever they could, slave families tried to stick together and hold onto their African customs.

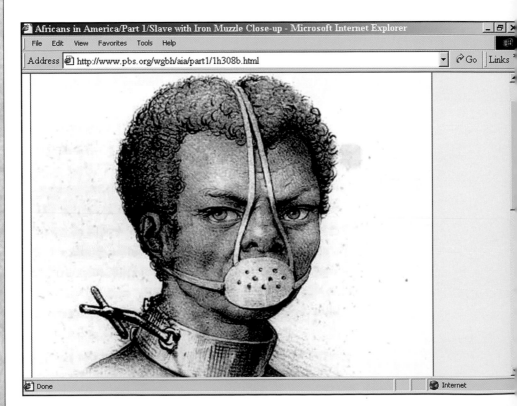

Africans in America/Part 1/Slave with Iron Muzzle Close-up - Microsoft Internet Explorer

File   Edit   View   Favorites   Tools   Help

Address http://www.pbs.org/wgbh/aia/part1/1h308b.html   Go Links

Done   Internet

▲ *This disturbing illustration of a slave wearing an iron muzzle comes from an 1839 French publication. When some slaves were accused by their masters of disobeying them, or eating too much food, they were made to wear these cruel and inhuman devices.*

Grandparents, parents, children, aunts, uncles, and cousins all would be welcome in the family group—with the elders passing down stories and African chants to the children. When slaves were introduced to Christianity, those chants evolved into spirituals. If one member of the group had learned something valuable—either how to read or write or some information about a possible escape—he or she would pass it along to other slaves. Even young Frederick Douglass, as a twelve-year-old slave boy, found a way to learn. With his one book in hand, he would trade bread with the poor white boys he met on the street in exchange for their teaching him to read a few words. Douglass would become a famous antislavery speaker and writer.

▶ Conflicting Laws

After the nation gained its independence, some state governments began to question whether slavery should be continued where it already existed or expanded into the new territories. This resulted in laws both to uphold slavery and to abolish, or end, the practice. Tensions between the states grew.

Between 1777 and 1804, the citizens in most Northern states voted to abolish slavery immediately, with some states agreeing to emancipate, or free, the slaves gradually. In 1787, the Northwest Ordinance banned slavery in the Northwest Territory, which included the future states of Illinois, Indiana, Michigan, Ohio, and Wisconsin and the eastern part of Minnesota. Yet in 1793, the U.S. Congress established the first Fugitive Slave Law, which allowed slave owners to cross state lines to capture their slaves who had escaped. This meant that escaped slaves still were not safe from their former masters, even in

Northern states and territories that did not allow slavery. In response, Northern states passed anti-kidnapping laws, which punished people who kidnapped free blacks to make them slaves, rather than capture fugitive slaves.

Even though many people felt that slavery was wrong, racism against African Americans was widespread. Slaves were not even counted as whole people. Article 1 of the U.S. Constitution established the "three-fifths clause" in which only three fifths of the number of slaves in a state were counted toward its population for taxation and representation, while a free person was counted as one.

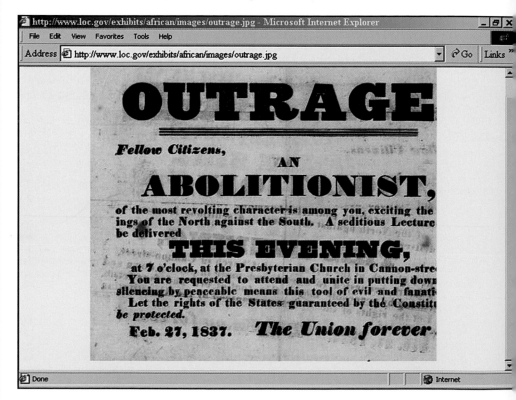

▲ Those who supported the institution of slavery were just as zealous in their beliefs as those who tried to abolish it. This handbill urged people who opposed the abolition of slavery to attend an antislavery meeting to unite "in putting down and silencing . . . this tool of evil and fanaticism."

The turn of the nineteenth century saw the beginning of efforts to strike a balance between Northern and Southern beliefs. In 1808, Congress banned the import of slaves from other countries, but allowed the purchase and sale of slaves who were already in the United States to continue. As the growing nation added new states, it tried to keep the balance. The Missouri Compromise of 1820 admitted Missouri as a slave state and Maine as a free state into the Union.

In 1821, some freed African-American slaves left the United States to start a new colony on the west coast of Africa. Many of these former slaves were given passage through money raised by a group known as the American Colonization Society. The society was founded in 1817 by white men who believed slavery was wrong but who also believed the best place for Africans was not America but Africa. Henry Clay, the leading figure behind the Missouri Compromise, shared this view, as did Abraham Lincoln for a time. About fifteen thousand former slaves settled in this colony between 1822 and 1861. In 1847, it became the independent nation of Liberia. Many African Americans did not like the idea of leaving their homeland, however, even though they suffered racism in America. By 1861, with the outbreak of the Civil War, immigration to Liberia came to a standstill.

▶ The Liberator

In January 1831, a white man named William Lloyd Garrison founded the antislavery newspaper *The Liberator*. Garrison believed that slavery was sinful and should be ended immediately. He opposed those who said that slaves should be emancipated gradually. The founding of Garrison's newspaper stirred the growing

http://www.loc.gov/exhibits/african/images/joseph.jpg - Microsoft Internet Explorer

File   Edit   View   Favorites   Tools   Help

Address http://www.loc.gov/exhibits/african/images/joseph.jpg   Go   Links

Done   Internet

▲ *Joseph Jenkins Roberts emigrated from Petersburg, Virginia, in 1829 to Monrovia, in West Africa, to live in a colony founded by the American Colonization Society. In 1848, when that colony became the independent nation of Liberia, he was elected its first president.*

abolitionist movement—the organized effort to abolish slavery in the United States.

For former slaves like Frederick Douglass, *The Liberator* was a powerful tool in the fight against slavery. "The paper became my meat and my drink," Douglass wrote later. ". . . Its sympathy for my brethren in bonds—its scathing denunciations of slaveholders—its faithful exposures of slavery—and its powerful attacks upon the upholders of the institution—sent a thrill of joy through my soul, such as I had never felt before!"[1]

Revolt and Mutiny

In the summer of 1831, a slave in Virginia named Nat Turner could not wait any longer. He had been having powerful visions that urged him to take up arms against his master. Other slaves looked up to Turner as a preacher, and they agreed to follow him in a slave revolt. On a dark August night, with about sixty followers, Turner killed the family of his owner and then turned on the neighborhood, killing fifty-five other white people. The revolt, which became known as Nat Turner's Rebellion, was quickly put down. Thirteen slaves and three free blacks were quickly hanged. Although Turner initially escaped, he was captured in late October and hanged as well.

In the aftermath of the rebellion, whites were terrified. Angry white mobs soon murdered about two hundred slaves, most of whom had not even been involved in Turner's revolt. The rebellion also led to calls for harsher slave codes as well as the end of some growing abolitionist efforts in the South. Yet abolitionists in the North became even more convinced that slavery needed to be brought to an end soon—either by new laws or by more bloodshed.

A few years later, in July 1839, African slaves mounted a brutal mutiny on the slave ship *La Amistad*, which was sailing around the coast of Cuba. Joseph Cinqué led a group of more than fifty slaves in a rebellion aboard ship, killing the captain and the cook. They allowed a Spanish navigator to live, hoping that he would sail them back to the coast of Africa. Instead, the navigator headed north to Long Island, New York, where the mutineers were captured. The mutiny led to court battles over whether the slaves should be allowed to go home to Africa. Eventually, the slaves won their case, and the thirty-five surviving

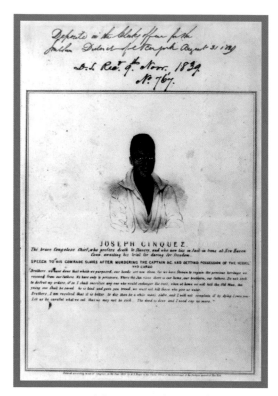

JOSEPH CINQUEZ.

Joseph Cinqué (or Cinquéz) was the leader of a group of fifty-three Africans who staged a revolt aboard the slave ship La Amistad. *They were eventually able to win their freedom in court thanks in large part to John Quincy Adams, the former U.S. president, who represented them.*

mutineers from *La Amistad* returned to Africa in January 1842.

▶ The Underground Railroad

Slaves opposed slavery in many ways. Some, like Nat Turner and Joseph Cinqué, led slave uprisings. Others chose to escape. Many used the Underground Railroad as their passageway. The Underground Railroad was not an actual railroad, but a secret network of safe houses, hidden passageways and codes, and daring guides who risked their lives to help slaves escape. Although the system began to bc used in the late eighteenth century, awareness of the Underground Railroad peaked around 1830 and continued through the outbreak of the Civil War.

The Underground Railroad included many escape routes. Most led to the northern United States and to Canada, although some slaves found routes south to Mexico or the Caribbean islands as well. Some slaves even found passage to Europe. For all, escape was scary and difficult. Fugitive slaves lived in fear of being recaptured

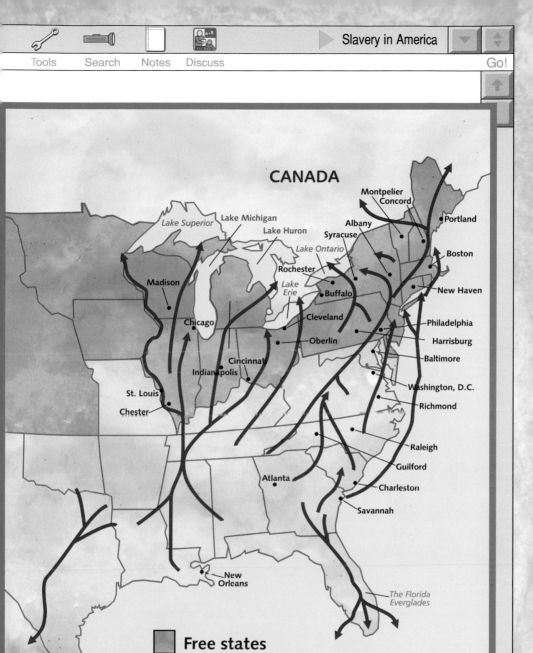

CANADA

Lake Superior   Lake Michigan

Lake Huron

Lake Ontario

Lake Erie

Montpelier
Concord
Albany
Syracuse
Rochester
Buffalo
Cleveland
Oberlin
Portland
Boston
New Haven
Philadelphia
Harrisburg
Baltimore
Washington, D.C.
Richmond

Madison

Chicago

Cincinnati
Indianapolis

St. Louis
Chester

Atlanta

Raleigh
Guilford
Charleston
Savannah

New
Orleans

The Florida
Everglades

Free states

Slave states

Caribbean Sea

MEXICO

▲ *This map shows the major routes of the Underground Railroad, which helped African Americans to escape slavery.*

by their masters. Although slaves followed generally understood routes, they often had to trust that their guides would safely show them the way to freedom. Their journeys would often zigzag across rivers and valleys and through thick forests and back roads.

The vast majority of brave people who helped slaves on the Underground Railroad are forgotten to history, but one would become famous: Harriet Tubman, a former slave and the Railroad's most well-known "conductor." After Tubman escaped from slavery in 1849, she returned to the South to help her family flee. She returned at least nineteen times, eventually rescuing more

Africans in America/Part 4/Portrait of Harriet Tubman Close-up - Microsoft Internet Explorer

File   Edit   View   Favorites   Tools   Help

Address http://www.pbs.org/wgbh/aia/part4/4h2961b.html

▲ *After escaping from slavery, Harriet Tubman became one of the most well-known "conductors" on the Underground Railroad, helping thousands to find freedom in the North and Canada.*

than three hundred slaves. Slaveholders heard about her successes and offered a $40,000 reward for her capture, but she dodged them each time.

▶ Hidden Codes

Although slaves often had to trust their conductors, many had a keen sense of direction themselves. From a young age, slaves were taught to locate the North Star in the sky, which pointed toward the free states. If skies were cloudy, slaves knew to look for moss, which tends to grow on the northern side of trees. Abolitionists and owners of safe houses also hung quilts in their windows that contained hidden information about directions and safe houses sewn into the panels.

Songs were also an important communication tool. Well-known spirituals such as "Wade in the Water" and "Steal Away" included hidden clues, such as wading in streams and creeks to erase one's scent so pursuing dogs would not be able to pick it up. Another spiritual was "Follow the Drinking Gourd." The gourd was a reference to the Big Dipper, with the North Star anchoring its handle. The spiritual "Swing Low, Sweet Chariot" was Harriet Tubman's favorite song. The chariot, mentioned in many spirituals, was a symbol for the Underground Railroad. The song also referred to the Jordan River, which was actually a code name for the Ohio River, a border between free states and border states. When Tubman died in 1913, "Swing Low, Sweet Chariot" was played in her honor:

> I look'd over Jordan, an' what did I see,
> Comin' for to carry me home.
> A band of angels comin' after me
> Comin' for to carry me home.

Africans in America/Part 4/A Ride for Liberty Close-up - Microsoft Internet Explorer

File   Edit   View   Favorites   Tools   Help

Address http://www.pbs.org/wgbh/aia/part4/4h1555b.html   Go   Links

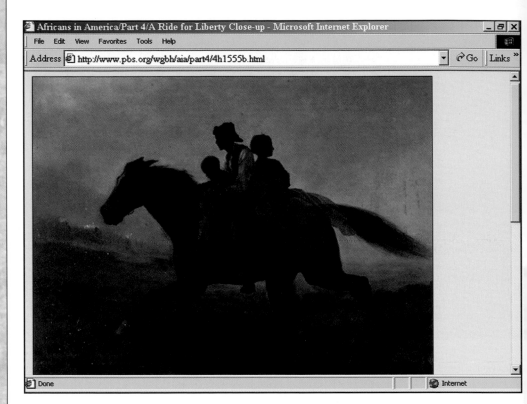

Done   Internet

▲ *In* A Ride for Liberty, *American painter Eastman Johnson recalled a scene he had witnessed during the Civil War. The black slave family is shown riding toward freedom, while the mother watches to see if they are being pursued.*

> Swing low sweet chariot
> Comin' for to carry me home.
> Swing low sweet chariot
> Comin' for to carry me home.[2]

As the nation moved closer to civil war, more and more slaves escaped through the Underground Railroad, riding the "sweet chariot" to freedom.

Slavery and the Civil War

By the middle of the nineteenth century, slavery was held even more firmly in place by federal laws. The United States was still expanding—which raised the question about whether slavery would be allowed in new states and territories. Continued debate on that question led to a series of bills known as the Compromise of 1850. These

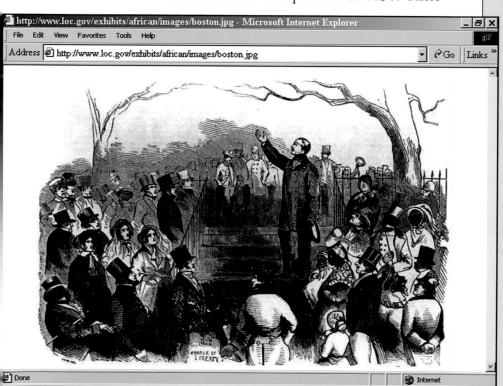

http://www.loc.gov/exhibits/african/images/boston.jpg - Microsoft Internet Explorer

File   Edit   View   Favorites   Tools   Help

Address http://www.loc.gov/exhibits/african/images/boston.jpg   Go   Links »

Done   Internet

▲ This engraving shows an August 1851 rally on Boston Common in which abolitionist Wendell Phillips protested the plight of Thomas Sims, a fugitive slave being tried in Boston. Despite Phillips' pleas, Sims was returned to Savannah, Georgia.

measures admitted California to the Union as a free state. But they also admitted new territory in which the question of slavery would be left up to the white settlers of those territories, in what was known as popular sovereignty.

The Compromise also allowed the South to tighten its grip on slavery with a second, stronger Fugitive Slave Law. Once again, slave catchers used the law as an excuse to kidnap free blacks. And again, the North responded by establishing penalties for kidnapping African Americans. Still, many blacks fled to Canada during this time rather than risk being kidnapped.

The nation became even more divided on the issue of slavery.

▶ *Uncle Tom's Cabin*

In 1851, an antislavery story began to appear as a regular series in an abolitionist newspaper. The next year, the series was published as a book, and the book became a rallying cry for abolitionists. The author was Harriet Beecher Stowe, who came from a family of staunch abolitionists, and the book was *Uncle Tom's Cabin*. Written by candlelight, after her six children went to sleep, Stowe's book was about a good-hearted slave and his struggles with a cruel master. It became an immediate best-seller, leading to more letters and articles calling for the end of slavery. During the years of the Civil War, when Harriet Beecher Stowe met Abraham Lincoln, the president jokingly remarked to her, "So you're the little woman who wrote the book that started this great war."[1]

▶ Trouble in Kansas

But things were getting worse for the abolitionists. The Kansas-Nebraska Act of 1854 established the territories

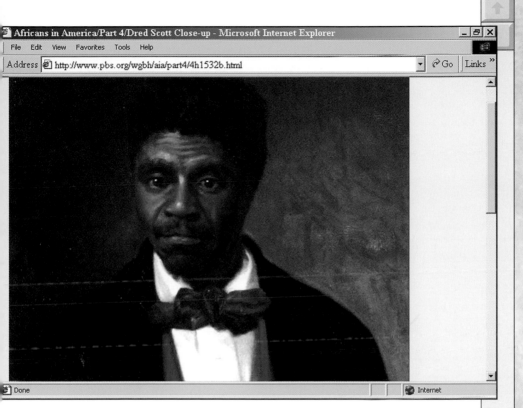

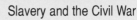

Africans in America/Part 4/Dred Scott Close-up - Microsoft Internet Explorer

File   Edit   View   Favorites   Tools   Help

Address http://www.pbs.org/wgbh/aia/part4/4h1532b.html   Go   Links »

Done   Internet

▲ *Dred Scott was fifty years old when he and his wife, Harriet, sued for their freedom in a St. Louis court. Their case was finally brought before the Supreme Court of the United States ten years later.*

of Kansas and Nebraska as territories where popular sovereignty would decide the question of slavery. The act repealed the Missouri Compromise ban on slavery north of a certain line of latitude. Two years later, a series of deadly clashes broke out between proslavery and abolitionist groups in Kansas. The brutal conflict became known as "Bleeding Kansas."

The next year, even the U.S. Supreme Court turned its back on the Missouri Compromise. In 1857, the Court decided the famous Dred Scott case. Scott was a

slave who had lived in the free North with his owner for several years. Scott argued that, as a citizen in a free state, he should be free. But the Court ruled that Scott was not a U.S. citizen. In addition to overturning the Missouri Compromise, the ruling stated that Scott, and all African Americans, had no civil rights under the Constitution and that slavery could not be banned in the new territories.

It was a heavy blow for abolitionists. But Frederick Douglass held on to hope. "We are now told . . . that the day is lost—all lost—and that we might as well give up the struggle. . . ." he said. "The voice of the Supreme Court has gone out over the troubled waves of the National Conscience . . . [But] my hopes were never brighter than now."[2]

▷ John Brown Takes Action

In 1859, a radical abolitionist named John Brown decided to take matters into his own hands. "Talk! Talk! Talk!" he exclaimed after an antislavery meeting. "That will never free the slaves. What is needed is action—action."[3] Gathering a band of men, Brown led a raid to steal weapons from a federal armory and arsenal in Harpers Ferry, Virginia. His goal was to arm slaves and start a slave rebellion.

Brown and his group easily entered the arsenal, but were unable to hold it. He and his men were caught and hanged for their crime. At first, many people considered Brown's actions those of a fanatic. But in his death, he became a symbol of sacrifice and a martyr for the abolitionist movement. After Harpers Ferry, many abolitionists vowed to fight slavery at all costs.

Abraham Lincoln's election in 1860 as the sixteenth president of the United States led to the South's secession and eventually the Civil War. Although Lincoln believed slavery to be an evil, his campaign promised to stem the spread of slavery, not threaten its very existence.

A House Divided

In 1860, the nation elected a new president, Abraham Lincoln. A lawyer from Illinois, Lincoln was known in his state for his antislav-ery beliefs and his truthfulness. He had even earned the nickname "Honest Abe." Lincoln believed that the nation's differences over slavery would tear it apart. When he won the Republican party's nomination for senator, Lincoln quoted the Bible in his acceptance speech, saying, "A house divided against itself cannot stand."[4] He was right, although he lost the Senate race to Stephen A. Douglas. A month following Lincoln's election as presi-dent, the citizens of South Carolina voted to leave, or secede from, the United States. By February 1861, six more states that had seceded joined with South Carolina to form the Confederate States of America. People feared that this withdrawal—called secession—would lead to civil war.

In April 1861, the first shots of the Civil War were fired on Fort Sumter, South Carolina. Lincoln called for troops to be mobilized for action, and thousands of men

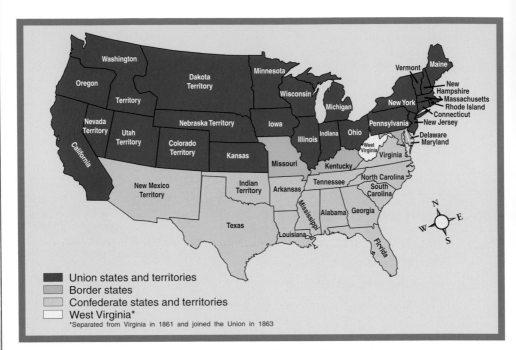

▲ This map shows the alignment of free, border, and slave states in the United States during the Civil War, 1861 to 1865.

responded. The South also began getting an army together. By the summer, the Union and Confederate armies began to clash on battlefields throughout Virginia.

For most soldiers who went off to war, slavery was not a driving factor. Many Union and Confederate soldiers felt that they were protecting their beliefs and way of life. Yet slavery was still a divisive political issue, even around the world. The Confederacy wanted Great Britain and France to recognize the Confederate States of America as a separate nation and support it with money and arms.

The war seemed to strengthen the Union government's backbone about slavery. In the spring of 1862, Congress banned slavery in the territories and abolished slavery in the District of Columbia.

Marching Orders

From the moment that war was declared, former slaves and freed African Americans wanted to join the fight. Black Americans had fought in the American Revolution and the War of 1812, but since then a federal law forbade blacks from serving in the military. Many groups of African Americans (then called "colored" or "Negroes") sent letters and petitions to President Lincoln. One group wrote: "We are strong in numbers, in courage, and in patriotism, and in behalf of our fellow countrymen of the colored race, we offer to you and to the nation a power and a will sufficient to conquer rebellion, and establish peace on a permanent basis."[5]

At first, the U.S. government argued that the Civil War was a "white man's war." Racism was a main cause of this feeling. Although most Northerners felt that slavery was wrong, they still did not believe that blacks were equal to whites. Most Northern white soldiers did not want to fight side by side with black soldiers. But the longer the war dragged on, the more the government realized that the army could use the manpower. In July 1862, Congress authorized Lincoln to enlist black military recruits. By the following spring, black regiments had formed both in the North and at Union outposts in the South.

President Lincoln had been thinking about emancipating the slaves for a long time. In the summer of 1862, Lincoln announced to his cabinet his plan to issue an emancipation proclamation. But the Union army had suffered a string of defeats on the battlefield, weakening Lincoln's position. His advisers urged him to wait for a major Union victory on the battlefield before releasing the proclamation.

Chapter 4 ▶

The Emancipation Proclamation

It was not long before Lincoln received the victory he needed to issue the Emancipation Proclamation. In September, feeling confident from his recent victories, Confederate General Robert E. Lee took his army north. The Confederates faced the Union army on a field near the town of Sharpsburg, Maryland. There, the two armies fought the one-day battle of Antietam (named for nearby Antietam Creek). The Confederates called it the Battle of Sharpsburg. With about twenty-three thousand soldiers dead, wounded, or missing after the battle, Antietam was the bloodiest single day of the Civil War. Although the Union army had suffered major losses, Lee's army had been forced to retreat to Virginia.

◀ This poster celebrates the signing of the Emancipation Proclamation, which went into effect on January 1, 1863. The proclamation allowed African Americans to enlist in the Union army and gave all Union soldiers an even greater reason to fight for the country's preservation.

Encouraged that the Union forces had held their ground, Lincoln issued a preliminary Emancipation Proclamation. The document stated that, as of January 1, 1863, slaves in the states then under rebellion "shall be then, thenceforward, and forever free."[1]

Forever Free

Although the Emancipation Proclamation is viewed as the document that freed the slaves, it did not actually free all slaves. The proclamation applied only to slaves in those states that were waging war against the Union. That meant that slaves in the territories and border states were not actually freed by the document. Many abolitionists were disappointed that the proclamation did not pledge to end all slavery.

But for many slaves and free blacks, the proclamation was the boldest antislavery action that the federal government had ever taken. The document was printed in full in several newspapers. In Washington, freed blacks were so excited that they tore the newspapers to shreds in their haste to read Lincoln's famous words. Henry M. Turner, a freed black in Washington, remembered the frenzy after the proclamation was released: "Men squealed, women fainted, dogs barked, white and colored people shook hands, [and] songs were sung. . . ."[2]

Even those unhappy with the proclamation's wording thought that, once slaves in the rebellious states were freed, it would not be long before slavery was ended everywhere. The proclamation also dealt a final blow to the South's hope for help from Great Britain and France, since neither European country would support the continuation of slavery.

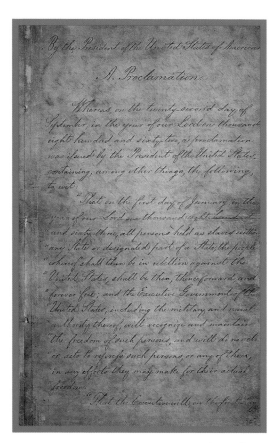

A draft of the proclamation's first page, in Lincoln's handwriting.

▶ Planning for Reconstruction

After Lincoln issued the Emancipation Proclamation, he quickly began to plan how to rebuild the nation after the Civil War. This period would become known as Reconstruction. In December 1863, Lincoln created the first Reconstruction Plan for the nation, proposing that Southern states be allowed to keep the governmental systems they had before the war.

By the summer of 1864, Congress passed the Wade-Davis bill, which would have required one half of a seceded state's white male citizens to swear their loyalty to the Constitution before a new state government could be formed. But Lincoln refused to sign the bill because he thought its terms were too harsh.

In March 1865, Congress created the Freedmen's Bureau, the first act of welfare for former slaves. It provided short-term relief to freed slaves, including basic shelter and medical care. About 4 million slaves were now a part of the free world, and the government was determined to help them.

Bravery on the Battlefield

Emancipation had led to the quick enlistment of nearly two hundred thousand African-American men in the Union army, as well as other blacks who also served as laborers, cooks, and carpenters for the army. The first major battle fought by black troops took place at Port Hudson, along the lower Mississippi River, in May 1863. Less than a month later, black regiments successfully beat back a Confederate attack on Milliken's Bend, a Union outpost near Vicksburg, Mississippi.

The most famous battle waged by African-American troops was fought at Fort Wagner, near Charleston, South Carolina. On July 18, 1863, the 54th Massachusetts, which included two sons of Frederick Douglass, led a charge against the fort. As they bravely attacked, the Confederates aimed round after round of musket fire at them. Still, most of the 54th made it over the fort's walls, where they fought hand to hand with the rebels. More than half of the regiment, including their white commander Robert Gould Shaw, was killed. But the 54th Massachusetts would be remembered as a symbol of the courage of black soldiers and their willingness to die for their country.

Black troops suffered even more than most soldiers. In addition to being given lowly tasks and being paid less than white soldiers, African-American soldiers were subject to racism in both the North and the South. At Fort Pillow, Tennessee, in 1864, dozens of black soldiers were murdered by Confederates even after they tried to surrender.

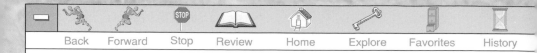

Africans in America/Part 4/ Close-up - Microsoft Internet Explorer

File Edit View Favorites Tools Help

Address http://www.pbs.org/wgbh/aia/part4/4h1526b.html Go Links

Done   Internet

The soldiers of Company E, 4th United States Colored Infantry. This black detachment was assigned to guard the nation's capital. Following the Emancipation Proclamation, the Union army began recruiting black soldiers, who would serve in large numbers, though in segregated units, through the remainder of the war.

That massacre made African-American soldiers even more ready to fight. In the last year of war, more and more black regiments were formed and sent into battle. Black troops played a vital role in the long, final campaign to gain control of the Confederate capital at Richmond, Virginia, and the nearby town of Petersburg. Eventually, the exhausted Confederate army had to retreat to a small village called Appomattox Court House.

Joy and Pain

By the spring of 1865, the Confederate army was feeling desperate. The Confederate government even promised to free slaves if they would join the rebel forces. Although several Confederate black regiments were formed, none ever saw battle, because the war was nearly over. In April, sitting in the parlor of a home in Appomattox Court House, Confederate general Robert E. Lee met with Union general Ulysses S. Grant to discuss the terms of surrender. Lee's surrender signaled the end of the Civil War, even though a few minor battles took place afterward.

When the news of Lee's surrender spread, joyous citizens—both black and white—celebrated the Union victory. A 500-gun salute took place in Washington, D.C. But the joyous celebration was cut short. A week later, President Lincoln and his wife were enjoying a play at Ford's Theatre in Washington when a deranged actor and Confederate sympathizer named John Wilkes Booth shot Lincoln in the head. Although Lincoln held on to life throughout the night, on the morning of April 15, the president died.

To African Americans, Lincoln's assassination marked a dark moment in an otherwise joyous time, since many believed that the president had paid for his antislavery beliefs with his life. "Sadness has taken hold of our hearts," wrote the New Orleans *Tribune*, an African-American newspaper. ". . . Lincoln and John Brown are two martyrs, whose memories will live united in our bosoms. Both have willingly jeopardized their lives for the sacred cause of freedom."[3]

Chapter 5

The Aftermath of Slavery

In the summer of 1865, a new president faced a nation in need of reuniting. In one of his first presidential acts, President Andrew Johnson implemented a reconstruction plan that required Southern states to approve the Thirteenth Amendment to the Constitution, which would ban slavery forever. At first, Southerners did not want to cooperate. But by December, the Thirteenth Amendment was ratified by the required number of states, and slavery was finally banned throughout the United States.

▶ Citizenship and Civil Rights

But the end of slavery did not mean that African Americans automatically were granted civil rights. A year after Lee's surrender at Appomattox, the Fourteenth Amendment was proposed but rejected. That amendment defined citizenship as belonging to all people born or naturalized in the United States. The amendment was finally ratified in July 1868.

Congress also passed several Reconstruction Acts during this time, which required Southern states to allow black men the right to vote. In March 1870, the Fifteenth Amendment, which protects voting rights for free blacks and former slaves, became part of the Constitution. For a brief period of time, blacks served in state and local governments throughout the South.

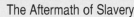

▲ *In Winslow Homer's* A Visit from the Old Mistress, *the artist captures the new and awkward relationship between former slaves and the plantation owners they once worked for.*

▶ The Ku Klux Klan

Despite these advances, the period of Reconstruction did not last. In the 1870s, Southern states were electing "redeemer" governments—which were white-only and opposed to racial equality. These efforts coincided with the rise of a secret group called the Ku Klux Klan. The Klan believed in white supremacy, or superiority, over African Americans, and its targets included members of the Republican party, who it believed were destroying the South. Wearing white hoods and robes, Klan members

used violence and terror, attacking blacks, killing them, and keeping others away from voting booths.

In April 1871, Congress passed the Ku Klux Klan Act, which forced the South to uphold the Fourteenth and Fifteenth Amendments. The act also allowed the U.S. government to punish people who committed acts of violence against blacks. But the attacks continued, and the Ku Klux Klan became more secretive than ever. The Klan, although in different form, became even more forceful in the early twentieth century, before losing power after the civil rights movement of the 1950s and 1960s. The Ku Klux Klan still exists as an organization that preaches white supremacy.

▶ Jim Crow and Segregation

By the end of the nineteenth century, the United States was almost as divided on the issue of race as it had been before the Civil War. In 1896, the Supreme Court made a

fateful decision in the *Plessy* v. *Ferguson* case. The ruling stated that separate but equal facilities for whites and blacks were allowed under the U.S.

◀ *Sarah Gudger was one hundred twenty-one years of age when she was interviewed in the 1930s about her childhood experiences as a slave.*

Constitution, making segregation legal. *Plessy* v. *Ferguson* encouraged the passage of laws to segregate railways, streetcars, public waiting rooms, restaurants, and even parks. Blacks were forced to use completely separate schools and hospitals, which were almost always in poorer condition than those used by whites. Although segregation was most pronounced in the South, it also existed in the North.

These laws became known as Jim Crow laws, named for a character in an old song who painted his face black and made fun of African Americans. Jim Crow laws would govern the South far into the twentieth century.

▶ The Civil Rights Movement

After World War II, African Americans found themselves struggling for equality again, almost exactly a century after the Civil War. In the 1950s and 1960s, the civil rights movement saw different types of battles, as African Americans fought for equal rights in voting and education. Civil rights leaders staged marches, gave speeches, and promoted equal rights for black Americans.

One of the defining moments of the civil rights movement was the March on Washington, D.C., for Civil Rights, held in August 1963. The most famous speaker that day was the Reverend Martin Luther King, Jr., one of the movement's leaders. Standing before the Lincoln Memorial, King drew a connection between slavery and segregation:

Fivescore years ago, a great American, in whose symbolic shadow we stand today, signed the Emancipation Proclamation. This momentous decree came as a great beacon light of hope to millions of Negro slaves. . . . But one hundred years later, the Negro still is not free; one hundred

◀ *The civil rights of African Americans were not guaranteed following the war. Dr. Martin Luther King and other civil rights leaders were still fighting for those rights nearly one hundred years later.*

years later, the life of the Negro is still sadly crippled by the manacles of segregation and the chains of discrimination. . . . One hundred years later, the Negro is still languished in the corners of American society and finds himself in exile in his own land.[1]

Although fighting for civil rights was often difficult and sometimes deadly—King himself was killed in 1968—the movement was ultimately successful. Passage of the Civil Rights Act of 1964, the Voting Rights Act of 1965, and the Fair Housing Act of 1968 finally ended the era of segregation—a system born out of slavery. King had hoped for such success. Speaking at the March on Washington, he pictured a day when all people could join hands and sing the words of an old Negro spiritual: "Free at last! Free at last; Thank God Almighty, we are free at last!"[2]

Chapter Notes

Chapter 1. Escaping to Freedom

1. Frederick Douglass, *Narrative of the Life of Frederick Douglass, an American Slave* with *Incidents in the Life of a Slave Girl by Harriet Jacobs* (New York: Modern Library, 2000), p. 251.

2. Ibid., p. 350.

Chapter 2. Slavery in America

1. Frederick Douglass, *Narrative of the Life of Frederick Douglass, an American Slave* with *Incidents in the Life of a Slave Girl by Harriet Jacobs* (New York: Modern Library, 2000), p. 106.

2. Jacqueline L.Tobin and Raymond G. Dobard, *Hidden in Plain View: A Secret Story of Quilts and the Underground Railroad* (New York: Doubleday, 1999), pp. 148–149.

Chapter 3. Slavery and the Civil War

1. Kenneth C. Davis, *Don't Know Much About the Civil War* (New York: Avon Books, 1996), p. 110.

2. Charles Johnson, Patricia Smith, and the WGBH Series Research Team, *Africans in America: America's Journey through Slavery* (New York: Harcourt Brace & Company, 1998), p. 419.

3. James M. McPherson, *Battle Cry of Freedom: The Civil War Era* (New York and Oxford: Oxford University Press, 1988), p. 203.

4. Ibid., p. 179.

5. James M. McPherson, *The Negro's Civil War: How American Blacks Felt and Acted During the War for the Union* (New York: Ballantine Books, 1991), p. 33.

Chapter 4. The Emancipation Proclamation

1. James M. McPherson, *Battle Cry of Freedom: The Civil War Era* (New York and Oxford: Oxford University Press, 1988), p. 557.

2. James M. McPherson, *The Negro's Civil War: How American Blacks Felt and Acted During the War for the Union* (New York: Ballantine Books, 1991), p. 50.

3. Ibid., p. 312.

Chapter 5. The Aftermath of Slavery

1. James M. Washington, ed., *A Testament of Hope: The Essential Writings and Speeches of Martin Luther King, Jr.* (New York: Harper Collins, 1986), p. 217.

2. Ibid., p. 220.

Further Reading

Bolotin, Norman. *Civil War A to Z: A Young Reader's Guide to Over 100 People, Places and Points of Importance.* New York: Dutton Children's Books, 2002.

Chang, Ina. *A Separate Battle: Women and the Civil War.* New York: Puffin Books, 1996.

Douglass, Frederick. *Narrative of the Life of Frederick Douglass, an American Slave* with *Incidents in the Life of a Slave Girl by Harriet Jacobs.* New York: Modern Library, 2000.

Fleischner, Jennifer. *I Was Born a Slave: The Story of Harriet Jacobs.* Brookfield, Conn.: Millbrook Press, 1997.

Fradin, Dennis Brindell. *Bound for the North Star: True Stories of Fugitive Slaves.* New York: Clarion Books, 2000.

Garrison, Mary. *Slaves Who Dared: The Stories of Ten African-American Heroes.* Shippensburg, Pa.: White Mane Kids, 2002.

Hamilton, Virginia. *Many Thousand Gone: African Americans From Slavery to Freedom.* New York: Knopf, 1993.

Holford, David M. *Lincoln and the Emancipation Proclamation in American History.* Berkeley Heights, N.J.: Enslow Publishers, Inc., 2002.

Johnson, Charles, Patricia Smith, and the WGBH Series Research Team. *Africans in America: America's Journey through Slavery.* New York: Harcourt Brace & Company, 1998.

McPherson, James M. *The Negro's Civil War: How American Blacks Felt and Acted During the War for the Union.* New York: Ballantine Books, 1991.

Index